MOVIE LOGIC

ALSO BY ERIK LA PRADE

Things Maps Don't Show
Del Mar, CA: Aegis Press, 1995

Figure Studies
New York: Linear Arts Books, 2000

SWATCHES
Hoboken, NJ: Poets Wear Prada, 2008

*BREAKING THROUGH: Richard Bellamy and The
Green Gallery, 1960–1965: Twenty-three Interviews*
New York: MidMarch Arts Press, 2010

False Confessions
Palo Alto, CA: Alternating Current (Propaganda Press),
2011

MOVIE LOGIC
POEMS

BY ERIK LA PRADE

POETS WEAR PRADA • Hoboken, New Jersey

MOVIE LOGIC: Poems

Poets Wear Prada
533 Bloomfield Street, Second Floor
Hoboken, New Jersey 07030

http://pwpbooks.blogspot.com

First North American Publication 2013.
First Mass Market Paperback Edition 2013.

Grateful acknowledgment is made to the following publications where some of these poems have appeared or are forthcoming:

Artist and Influence, The Hat, J Journal, Night Magazine, and *The Sienese Shredder.*

ISBN-13: 978-0615761237
ISBN-10: 0615761232

Printed in the U.S.A.

Front Cover Image: Robert Ghiradella

FOR

SPINNER;

LARAINE CHABERSKI'S CAT,

CHARLIE;

ABBEY KUPERSMITH'S & EDITH FRANK'S CAT,

CALLIE

TABLE OF CONTENTS

MOVIE LOGIC

"I told them that every experience meant something."
— **CHARLES BUKOWSKI**

"We all have it coming, kid."
— **WILLIAM MUNNY**
(Clint Eastwood), *Unforgiven* (1992)

AUDEN LIVED UPSTAIRS

I'm at Passport Restaurant,
Sitting at an outdoor table while
Eating a plate of couscous
And drinking an imported beer.
I'm facing 77 Saint Mark's
Place. A tourist walks up
The stoop to photograph Auden's
Memorial plaque, but it has been removed.
The only thing for him to look at is
A white outline that stains the red bricks;
He photographs the wall as his wife stands
On the bottom step shouting for him to come down,
Afraid he'll be arrested,
When an anonymous voice from the hallway
Calls out, "*Licitum est.*"

SHAYS'S REBELLION

I'm walking on a country road,
Past a farmhouse with a cornfield.
Two hundred years ago, some men
Died here, fighting for
The land they lived on.

There are no gravestones,
Only an iron plaque marks
The ground. I stand by a fence
Reading the legend.

My friend, Ben Gardner,
Waits for me to finish,
So we can walk back to his
Ancestor's house, half-a-mile away.

Ben is a Yale graduate, living here.
Since leaving college,
He's had five breakdowns.
In the mornings, he cleans
Toilets at a rehab for convicts.

In the afternoons, he reads
The Old Testament,
Then takes long walks with me.
In the evenings, we drink beer,
Talk, or read the books from
His grandmother's library.

"CRASH MAIL"

This describes a special category of debris
That family members and collectors
Seek from a catastrophe
Ending up in plastic envelopes:

Like the Hindenburg mail
From Lakehurst, New Jersey,
Franked with waterstains and burnmarks,
Now an expensive artifact
Found in collectors' ephemera albums;

Or the mail that survived Pan Am Flight 107
Over Lockerbie, Scotland,
Valued according to market demands;
Or the letters that fell on bungalows
In Rockaway, New York, from the explosion
Of American Airlines Flight 587.

TALKING TO EACH OTHER

I don't remember exactly why you left me;
But I kept the letter you sent three
Days later and read it. That's when
I called you. I had a tape recorder
Next to the phone receiver to play
Back the words of our conversation.
Nothing you could say ever sounded
Important enough to make me agree
With you. Then I rewound the tape
And listened to it again, thinking I'd
Call you back and tell you something
Different, assuming we met again,
Or I'd just give you the tape
And let you decide. But I never did.

EDGE NOTE
For Karen Adler

Some painters leave the
Edges of their canvas unpainted.
(See Monet's *Waterlillies*, for example.)
Do they like all those raw corners and white surfaces?
Some writers, too, use white space,
Say more with it than with words.
I write on scraps of paper and wind up
Losing half of them.

TEA DRUNK

The minerals in the tea are strong.
My face is flushed and there is
A buzz in my eyes. I'm drinking
A tea fired in May 2011 — Oolong,
Also known as Cliff tea.
Before each offering,
My host pours it into a glass,
Then spills it into a large ceramic bowl.
The tea is "sacrificing itself," he tells me.
I'm drinking my seventh cup, and after
A sip, he says, "inhale."
I feel the moisture in my mouth
Dry up and then return.

IN THE MIDDLE OF SOMETHING

I was cleaning under my bed
When I found two poems
Written three years ago. One poem
Was for a woman I loved — so I kept.
The other poem was for a woman
I also loved, but I ripped up the page and
Threw pieces out my window.
I didn't want to remember her
Because she hurt me in a good way.
Now, between the two of them,
I've written this as a statement
Of the obvious.

THREE T'ANG POETS

I
Summer in the city:
The morning is the best time
To take a walk, before a heat wave
Blankets the air, or battalions of
Pedestrians going to work
Crowd the streets, or
Police make random bag
Searches for terrorist bombs.

II
An old girlfriend
Has returned to her husband.
In her last letter, she wrote how
Sick he is from taking drugs,
But her children are there.
I miss having sex with her,
Even now, a year later.

III
I'm trying to remember
How long I've lived
In my current apartment.

As I count the neighbors who
Have died, I realize I'd better
Move to another apartment.

LATE NIGHT JAZZ ON THE RADIO

My girlfriend likes to sleep over when
There's a birthday tribute to a great musician
Like Armstrong, Jelly Roll Morton,
Teddy Wilson or Buck Clayton.
She takes off her clothes and we order in:
Chinese food, or sometimes Thai.

BALLAD OF A WEEKEND

I

I remember what you wrote,
As the sound of your voice
Fills the room tonight
With sudden memories.

Your cryptic apologies
Are ridiculous now,
As when you spoke of faults
In the Earth, or of an ice age

Alive with controversy:
How buried borders
Would suddenly surface
To cover us in shapeless

Earth, the landscape
Itself moving,
Shaking down the walls
Of our room with the dust

Of timbers.
"The mind has mountains," you said,
Quoting Hopkins. But, when the night
Folded itself into napkins of light,

I still didn't want to read your letter,
Or, even, clean up the scattered pieces
From the floor, and so left them
Lying in the gray sand.

II

In the bedroom's fireplace,
The fire that burned Rome
Glows: a red shadow,
Reflected in the old clock's glass face,
Turning time to diamond-hard memory.

Nearby, a violin hangs on the wall;
Its broken strings, like *crèche* angels, implore us
To repent from our morning lust,
And save ourselves from old faults.

III

Sailing, we drift in a haze of water …
Blue Chinese waves on porcelain.
Fuck your analyst!
I don't want you to understand me,

Or give me a lecture
On the language of the senses —
Not while the breeze is cool on my skin
And I can watch you sunbathe nude.

BUDDHA IN MY POCKET

I bought it from a street-fair vendor
Who sells Chinese artifacts he gets from China.
Two weeks later, I went back to browse
His tables again. I stood next to a Black man,
Who also searched among the trays
Of relics and hand-carved bone Buddhas.
I forget now what we talked about,
But he told me how he carried one
During the four years he
Toured Vietnam. He put his hand in
His pocket, took out his Buddha and showed it to me.
I took out my Buddha and showed it to him,
Then we both laughed and walked in opposite directions.

MYTH MAKING

I got up at 6:06 a.m. this morning,
Bought two newspapers and coffee
After walking the dog. By eight o'clock,
I'm finished with the world and its
Newsprint obituaries, fashion trends,
Politics, movie reviews and falling
Stocks. While the world moves
In one direction, I move in another,
Trying to contrive some mundane
Conceit more interesting than
The newsprint that stains
My fingers. Directed by a habit
For cleanliness, I wipe my fingers
Off, using a page from my notebook
As a rag. Now, the ink is smudged —
Twice — and the world's influences
Are made into a tangible
Form on paper, something I can
Shape according to my whim:
Self-portrait with World, as an
Old Master might title it, ready
To be framed or sold, according
To the fashionable tastes of The Market.

THIS COULD BE YOU
For Joseph and Lauren

Your father is getting married
For the second time. Both
Families are together — drinking,
Dancing, talking, and looking.
The groom is color blind.
The bride's dress is orange,
So he can see it.
On the lawn, a mother-in-law sits
In an orange Datsun Z28, a replica
Of her daughter's first car —
A wedding gift;
She is driving in a circle, drunk.

NEW YEAR'S SECRET

On Sunday afternoons, the old Chinese
Fortune readers hang red cloths on the gated
Metal entrance to Confucius Park, Chinatown.
Since they speak no English, they each have
A woman to translate questions.
Most of the readers are refugees from
Pre-Mao China. Too old after World War II
To be reeducated, they would have disappeared
Had they owned land or houses,
Or dabbled in superstition.
I stand by the entrance, looking at their faces,
As several of them offer to read my palm.
Their pet songbirds, housed in wooden cages,
Sit on the lawn. Occasionally, the birds' songs
Mix with the sounds of men playing mah-jongg
At nearby chess tables. After twenty
Minutes, it costs me ten dollars to learn
I'll live to be eighty-six.

FOUR POEMS FOR SIDNEY LANIER

I

It's four o'clock in the morning
In Montgomery, Alabama, and I'm
Staying in a motel room. I've come
To visit the graves of people
Buried in Wetumpka,
A small town twenty miles from here.
But now, I'm waiting for a woman
To come out of the bathroom
And get into bed. Lorenzo, a cabdriver
I met in the airport, gave me her phone number.
The film on the cable channel
I'm watching is *Independence Day*,
A movie about a Black and a Jew
Who save the world from aliens —
A true metaphor for the South.

II

This morning I'm in the state archives,
Looking at slave schedules from 1860;
Not one has a name, just ages and letters for
Male or female. I can't read the
Handwriting and the 1890 census report
Was destroyed in a fire.
I'm getting tired of trying to read about the past
And its collection of records, deeds,
Census reports, births, deaths, old newspaper
Articles, and the things people did to survive —
Or to destroy themselves.

This afternoon I plan to visit Old Alabama Town,
A collection of nineteenth-century cabins
And wood-frame houses: a
Disneyland of Southern history,
Fenced off to keep the ghosts in.

III

Mid-August. Here, at the confluence of the Coosa and
The Tallapoosa, the Alabama River forms.
West of the river is the city cemetery, where
My people are buried. The oldest
Graves in Section G have no names or stones,
Only humps of rock sticking up from the ground.
Other names are recorded in the cemetery books.
The sun is hot and I don't have a hat.
My great aunt walks back to the car
While I stand here, reading the tombstone
Of a much-named nine-year old girl —
"Henry Ritter," "Ema Ritter," "Dema Ritter,"
"Sweet Potatoe," "Creamatarter," real name:
"Caroline Bostick" — dead before
I was born. Her gravestone nicknames are
Scratched over like grooves on
A wax cylinder. My father recited those
Names to me when I was a kid.
Now, I can almost hear
The voices of schoolchildren echoing
Among the graves.

My aunt has lived her whole life in this small town,
And only escaped dying young with the
Help of a White lawyer.
Nothing I write now will
Change how these people — Black or White —
Lived their small-town lives.
Sweat covers my forehead. I need a drink.

IV

At three a.m. a nightmare startles me awake
And into an anxiety attack;
I can't catch my breath — gasping for air —
As I sit at the desk
In the middle of the room.
My T.V. mind
Racing with details
Of some racial memory
As I try to write the dream down:

First, the crowd lynches his wife,
Then they call him to come out
To help them skin a cow. He says,
"Let me get a sheet to wrap it in."
So they let him go back inside the house.
He comes back out with a shotgun,
Killing four or five of them — before they get him.

The South is burying its past
Under the historical heading of *Tourism*,
But not all the bodies are buried
In the ground or hidden in family closets.
Moving back-and-forth between the bed
And the desk — the past and the present —
I am scaffolded, waiting
To shed my skin like an alien.

I'm leaving at six a.m. and it's still dark outside,
The streets dimly lit by traffic lights
As *Independence Day* continues playing
Twenty-four hours a day.

21

BALLOONS AND MOUNTAINS

Mother, the view from your hospital
Window is dangerous — high and steep —
With no visible places to grab:
Neither to ascend nor descend.
Your fingers and toes are red-blue
Like the final stages of frostbite that
Climbers on Mt. Everest suffer from.

With the invention of the hot air balloon,
It became possible to ascend to great heights,
Rapidly, without physical exertion.

You have chemicals and machines to help
You survive under your white sheet tent:
Seven bags, suspended by wire rods,
Continuously emptying their contents
Into your body.

The meteorologists Coxwell and Glaisher
Ascended 29,000 feet in a balloon to
Obtain samples of the air for analysis.
Both were overcome. Coxwell, after
Temporarily losing the use of his limbs,
Was able to use his teeth to pull the cord
That released some hydrogen from the balloon
And brought them down safely.

The nurse checks your numbers
As the air is pumped into your lungs at
An even rate. She tells me these
Are the best blood gas results, so far.

TRAIN NO. 17 CROSSES BRIDGE 201, WURNO SIDING, C. 1957

After the Photograph by O. Winston Link

Norfolk and Western Engine #601
Runs over a bridge,
Crossing the New River at night.

The engineer leans out of the window,
Looking straight ahead —
While a trail of white smoke
Replaces the horizon.

Below the bridge —
A man drives a 1955 Buick,
Following the road as it turns right.
His face is blurred.
He is about to leave the photograph,
Going somewhere. Maybe going home —
Or leaving it.

IN FOR THE NIGHT

The radio predicts evening rains
Followed by thunderstorms,
Ending my plans for a walk.

I need to stay home, anyway.
Write some letters. Clean my floor.
Then there is laundry to do.
And reading sections
From two-day old newspapers
Saved for certain articles.

Even spraying alcohol
On my bedsheets to ward off
Bedbugs is less stressful
Than crossing Eighth Avenue.

The weatherpeople got it wrong —
It hasn't rained for two hours.
I stare out the window as
The lights from the Empire State Building
Come on, coloring the clouds
Like smoke from incense —
Soft red, blue, yellow.

MOVIE LOGIC
For John McWhinnie (1968–2012)

Narrative and plot don't move
In the same time frame. Jump cuts
Cue up style and motive.

The director's vision arcs
Through everything, apparent
When some coincidence or deliberate
Accident makes an exit or sparks

Disaster. Is it cinematic truth
Or our own suspension of disbelief
We're watching? It doesn't matter.
We sit here awaiting the inevitable.

~THE END~

ACKNOWLEDGMENTS

The author extends his thanks to the following publications:

"Auden Lived Upstairs," "Myth Making"	*The Sienese Shredder*, #3, 2009
"Ballad of a Weekend"	*The Hat*, #8
"Talking to Each Other"	*Artist and Influence*, Vol. XXVI, 2007
"Buddha in My Pocket"	*Artist and Influence*, Vol. XXVIII, 2009
"Four Poems for Sidney Lanier"	*Artist and Influence*, Vol. XXIX, 2010
"Shays's Rebellion," "Balloons and Mountains"	*Night Magazine*, No. 38
"Tea Drunk"	*J Journal*, Fall 2012

ABOUT THE AUTHOR

Erik La Prade received his B.A. and M.A. from City College. His most recent poetry collection, a chapbook titled *False Confessions*, was published by Alternating Current in 2011. *Breaking Through: Richard Bellamy and The Green Gallery, 1960–1965*, published in 2010 by MidMarch Arts Press, traces the history of Dick Bellamy's celebrated art gallery through interviews with twenty-three of its exhibited artists including Claes Oldenberg, James Rosenquist, and Frank Stella. Poets Wear Prada issued a chapbook, *SWATCHES,* in 2008. Erik's first book, *Things Maps Don't Show*, was published in 1995; his second, *Figure Studies*, in 1999. His poems have appeared in *Artist and Influence, Fish Drum, The Hat, Night Magazine, The Reading Room*, and *The New York Times*. He has also published articles and interviews in *The Brooklyn Rail, Captured: A Film/Video History of The Lower East Side*, and *The Outlaw Bible of American Essays*.

www.ingramcontent.com/pod-product-compliance
Lightning Source LLC
Chambersburg PA
CBHW061759040426
42447CB00011B/2378